FUN FACT FILE: THE HISTORY OF HOLIDAYS

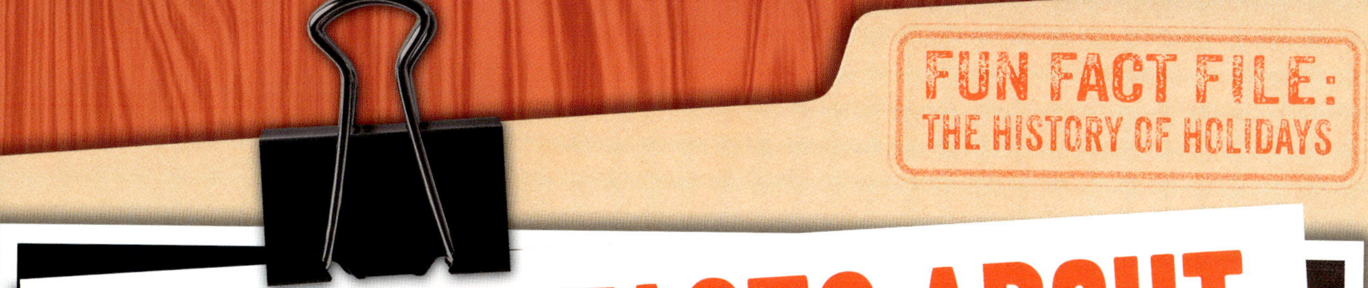

20 FUN FACTS ABOUT INDEPENDENCE DAY

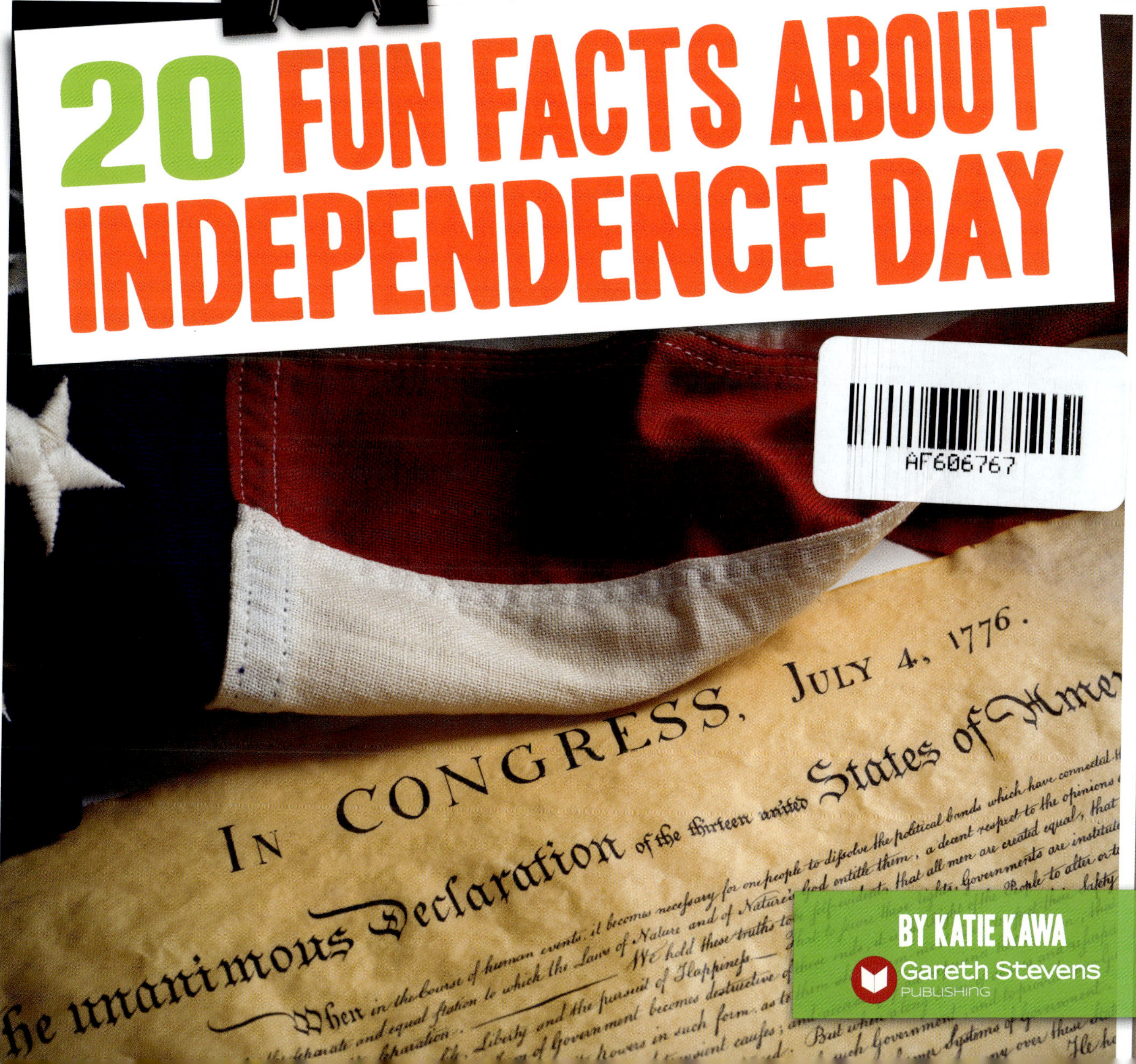

BY KATIE KAWA

Gareth Stevens PUBLISHING

Please visit our website, www.garethstevens.com. For a free color catalog of all our high-quality books, call toll free 1-800-542-2595 or fax 1-877-542-2596.

Library of Congress Cataloging-in-Publication Data
Names: Kawa, Katie, author.
Title: 20 fun facts about Independence Day / Katie Kawa.
Other titles: Twenty fun facts about Independence Day
Description: Buffalo, NY : Gareth Stevens Publishing, [2025] | Series: Fun fact file : the history of holidays | Includes bibliographical references and index.
Identifiers: LCCN 2024000190 (print) | LCCN 2024000191 (ebook) | ISBN 9781482466195 (library binding) | ISBN 9781482466188 (paperback) | ISBN 9781482466201 (ebook)
Subjects: LCSH: Fourth of July–Juvenile literature. | Fourth of July celebrations–Juvenile literature.
Classification: LCC E286 .A13835 2025 (print) | LCC E286 (ebook) | DDC 394.2634–dc23/eng/20240207
LC record available at https://lccn.loc.gov/2024000190
LC ebook record available at https://lccn.loc.gov/2024000191

First Edition

Published in 2025 by
Gareth Stevens Publishing
2544 Clinton St
Buffalo, NY 14224

Editor: Therese Shea

Photo credits: Cover, p. 1 (main) Mike Flippo/Shutterstock.com; file folder used throughout David Smart/Shutterstock.com; binder clip used throughout luckyraccoon/Shutterstock.com; wood grain background used throughout ARENA Creative/Shutterstock.com; p. 5 AS photo family/Shutterstock.com; p. 6 (Declaration) ungvar/Shutterstock.com; p. 6 (wood background) stockphoto mania/Shutterstock.com; p. 7 Gilbert Stuart, John Adams, c. 1800-1815, NGA 42933.jpg/Wikimedia Commons; p. 8 Writing the Declaration of Independence 1776 cph.3g09904.jpg/WIkimedia Commons; p. 9 f11photo/Shutterstock.com; pp. 10, 13, 20 (right) courtesy of the Library of Congress; p. 11 Textless map of territorial growth 1775.svg/WIkimedia Commons; p. 12 Sean Pavone/Shutterstock.com; p. 14 Keith J Finks/Shutterstock.com; p. 16 Frederick Douglass (circa 1879).jpg/Wikimedia Commons; p. 17 Aaron of L.A. Photography/Shutterstock.com; p. 18 lazyllama/Shutterstock.com; p. 19 White House Photograph Courtesy Gerald R. Ford Library; p. 20 (left) Official Presidential portrait of Thomas Jefferson (by Rembrandt Peale, 1800).jpg/Wikimedia Commons; p. 21 Zachary Taylor by Joseph Henry Bush, c1848.jpg/Wikimedia Commons; p. 22 Joseph Sohm/Shutterstock.com; p. 23 (flag) phloxii/Shutterstock.com; p. 23 (inset) Maridav/Shutterstock.com; p. 24 K2 PhotoStudio/Shutterstock.com; p. 25 a katz/Shutterstock.com; p. 26 Heather Forer/Shutterstock.com; p. 27 Marat Valiakhmetov/Shutterstock.com; p. 29 Monkey Business Images/Shutterstock.com.

Printed in the United States of America

CPSIA compliance information: Batch #CS25GS: For further information contact Gareth Stevens, New York, New York at 1-800-542-2595.

CONTENTS

Words in the glossary appear in **bold** type the first time they are used in the text.

WHY THE FOURTH OF JULY?

Every year on July 4, Americans gather to have picnics, watch fireworks, and enjoy time with family and friends. The Fourth of July is a day to **celebrate** across the United States, but what are people celebrating?

The answer is found in the official name of the holiday: Independence Day. On this day, Americans remember when the United States became an independent country in 1776. There are so many fun Fourth of July facts to learn—so let's get started!

Independence Day, or the Fourth of July, is a time for fun. Its history goes back to the American Revolution, the war in which the 13 British colonies in eastern North America won their freedom.

A DIFFERENT DAY

FUN FACT: 1

Although Americans celebrate July 4 as Independence Day, the Second **Continental Congress** voted for independence two days earlier. It was on July 2, 1776, that American leaders voted to separate from Great Britain.

After the Second Continental Congress voted for independence, they needed to approve, or agree on, the words that would declare it. On July 4, they approved the wording of the Declaration of Independence, shown here.

If John Adams had been correct, we'd be celebrating the Second of July as a holiday! Adams later became the second U.S. president.

FUN FACT: 2

JOHN ADAMS GUESSED THE WRONG DATE FOR THE NATIONAL CELEBRATION!

John Adams wrote to his wife Abigail that "the Second Day of July . . . will be celebrated." He thought Americans would celebrate the day that the Second Continental Congress voted for independence.

THE WORDS WE CELEBRATE

FUN FACT: 3

A FUTURE PRESIDENT WROTE THE DECLARATION OF INDEPENDENCE.

The Second Continental Congress chose a group of five men to write the Declaration of Independence. They were called the Committee of Five. The writing was done mostly by Thomas Jefferson. He became the third U.S. president.

This painting shows Thomas Jefferson (right) working with Benjamin Franklin (left) and John Adams (center) on the Declaration of Independence. The other two men chosen to create the **document** were Robert R. Livingston and Roger Sherman.

The Second Continental Congress met in Philadelphia, Pennsylvania, at what's now known as Independence Hall, shown here.

FUN FACT: 4

AFTER THE DECLARATION OF INDEPENDENCE WAS WRITTEN, ALMOST 100 CHANGES WERE MADE TO IT.

Some changes were made by the Committee of Five. More were made by the rest of the Second Continental Congress. At least 86 changes were made to the document in all.

FROM COLONIES TO STATES

FUN FACT: 5

NEW YORK COULD CELEBRATE INDEPENDENCE DAY ON JULY 9.

Twelve of the thirteen colonies voted for independence on July 2. New York didn't vote. Seven days later, on July 9, 1776, New York leaders approved the Declaration of Independence.

New York's **delegates** at the Second Continental Congress didn't vote on July 2, 1776, because they hadn't heard from the New York Congress about how to vote.

These 13 British colonies became the first 13 states in the United States of America.

EARLY CELEBRATIONS

FUN FACT: 6

NO BIG CELEBRATIONS HAPPENED ON JULY 4, 1776.

You might think the first Independence Day was a major cause for celebration. However, news traveled much slower in 1776 than it does today. The first public celebration of independence happened on July 8.

On July 8, 1776, the Declaration of Independence was read out loud in Philadelphia. Music was played and bells were rung. The Liberty Bell, shown here, may have been rung on this special day.

Shown here is an artist's take on the wild gathering of colonists in New York who pulled down King George's statue.

FUN FACT: 7

EARLY INDEPENDENCE CELEBRATIONS GOT WILD!

When the Declaration of Independence was first read in New York City, people pulled down a **statue** of the British king, George III. The metal from the statue was used to make balls that could be fired from guns called muskets.

A NATIONAL HOLIDAY

FUN FACT: 8

IT TOOK ALMOST 100 YEARS FOR INDEPENDENCE DAY TO BECOME A NATIONAL HOLIDAY.

The first official Fourth of July celebrations happened in 1777. In 1870, the U.S. Congress passed a law that made Independence Day a federal, or national, holiday.

In 1781, Massachusetts became the first state to make Independence Day an official state holiday. An Independence Day celebration in Boston, Massachusetts, is shown here.

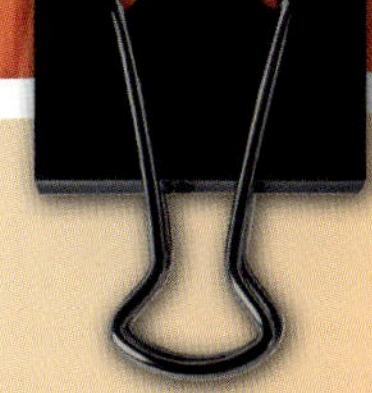

THE HISTORY OF INDEPENDENCE DAY

JULY 2, 1776	The Second Continental Congress votes to declare independence from Great Britain.
JULY 4, 1776	The Second Continental Congress approves and adopts the Declaration of Independence.
JULY 8, 1776	Celebrations of independence are held in Philadelphia.
JULY 9, 1776	New York officially adopts the Declaration of Independence.
JULY 4, 1777	The first **anniversary** of the Declaration of Independence is celebrated.
JULY 3, 1781	Massachusetts becomes the first state to make Independence Day an official holiday.
JUNE 28, 1870	Independence Day becomes a federal holiday.

Knowing the history of Independence Day can make celebrating it even more special.

FREEDOM FOR ALL?

FUN FACT: 9

SOME AMERICANS DIDN'T CELEBRATE INDEPENDENCE DAY—FOR A REASON.

In 1852, Frederick Douglass, a Black man who escaped **enslavement**, gave a speech called "What to the Slave Is the Fourth of July?" He said the day wasn't for all Americans, because not all Americans were free.

In his speech, Douglass said, "This Fourth of July is yours, not mine." He wanted Americans to understand that the rights and freedoms in the Declaration of Independence didn't exist for enslaved people.

Juneteenth celebrations, such as the one shown here, have been happening since 1865. This day became a federal holiday in 2021.

FUN FACT: 10

JUNETEENTH IS A DAY THAT CELEBRATES INDEPENDENCE TOO.

On June 19, 1865, after the end of the **American Civil War**, enslaved people in Galveston, Texas, learned they were free. June 19—also known as Juneteenth—is sometimes known as the "second Independence Day" of the United States.

WHAT ABOUT THE BRITISH?

FUN FACT: 11

THE UNITED STATES WAS THE FIRST BRITISH TERRITORY TO DECLARE INDEPENDENCE FROM ENGLAND.

However, it was far from the last. Since then, around 60 countries have gained independence from the United Kingdom (England, Scotland, Wales, and Northern Ireland).

The United Kingdom holds the record for being the country from which the most countries have declared independence.

Queen Elizabeth II of England danced with U.S. President Gerald Ford in July 1976. This would have been unimaginable to King George III in 1776!

FUN FACT: 12

THE BRITISH QUEEN CELEBRATED INDEPENDENCE DAY IN THE UNITED STATES.

In 1976, the United States celebrated its bicentennial, or its 200th anniversary, of independence. That year, Queen Elizabeth II of England visited the White House on July 7 as a part of the celebration.

A DANGEROUS DAY FOR PRESIDENTS

FUN FACT: 13

THREE U.S. PRESIDENTS HAVE DIED ON JULY 4.

John Adams (the second president) and Thomas Jefferson (the third president) both died on the exact same day—July 4, 1826. James Monroe (the fifth president) died a few years later, on July 4, 1831.

Jefferson (left) and Adams (right) died exactly 50 years after the Declaration of Independence was approved.

Some people believe Zachary Taylor got sick from the water or milk he drank at the celebration. Others believe cherries he ate made him sick.

FUN FACT: 14

INDEPENDENCE DAY CELEBRATIONS MAY HAVE KILLED A PRESIDENT!

President Zachary Taylor died on July 9, 1850, after only being in office for 16 months. He got sick after attending Fourth of July celebrations in Washington, DC, and died days later.

SPECIAL CELEBRATIONS

FUN FACT: 15

INDEPENDENCE DAY IS ALSO NATIONAL BELL RINGING DAY.

In 1963, the U.S. Congress and President John F. Kennedy declared July 4 would be National Bell Ringing Day. This honors how bells were rung to celebrate independence in the early years of U.S. history.

The 1963 act of Congress states that bells are to be rung 13 times at 2:00 p.m. on July 4. Many places across the United States do this, including the Old North Church in Boston, Massachusetts, shown here.

HONOLULU, HAWAII

FUN FACT: 16

JULY 4 IS THE DAY NEW STARS ARE ADDED TO THE U.S. FLAG.

When a new state is added to the United States, a new star is added to the U.S. flag **design**. This happens on the July 4 after the state joins the country.

A FAVORITE FOOD

FUN FACT: 17

AMERICANS EAT ABOUT 150 MILLION HOT DOGS ON INDEPENDENCE DAY.

Hot dogs are a popular food on Independence Day. In fact, the number of hot dogs Americans eat on this holiday would stretch from Los Angeles, California, to Washington, DC, more than five times!

Americans eat more hot dogs on Independence Day than any other day of the year according to the National Hot Dog and Sausage Council.

FUN FACT: 18

THE RECORD FOR THE MOST HOT DOGS AND BUNS EATEN IN 10 MINUTES IS 76!

Every July 4, a famous hot dog eating contest is held in New York City. In 2021, Joey Chestnut ate a record 76 hot dogs. As of 2023, he's won the contest 16 times.

LIGHTING UP THE SKY

FUN FACT: 19

Fireworks are a big part of Independence Day celebrations in the United States. They were invented in China around 200 BCE. The **technology** traveled to Europe and later to the United States.

The first anniversary of the Declaration of Independence in 1777 was celebrated with fireworks. But early fireworks were only one color—orange!

It's often more fun—and safer—to attend a town's or city's fireworks display. Fireworks set off at home cause a lot of injuries each year.

FUN FACT: 20

AMERICANS SPEND BILLIONS OF DOLLARS ON FIREWORKS EVERY YEAR.

Many Americans love to watch fireworks on Independence Day. Americans spent $2.3 billion on fireworks in 2023! Most fireworks set off on Independence Day come from China—the place where they were first invented.

AN IMPORTANT HOLIDAY

The United States isn't the only country that celebrates an Independence Day. All around the world, different nations celebrate the day they became independent. These holidays are important times to celebrate freedom and national **unity**.

In the United States, Independence Day is a holiday to remember our past. It also invites us to build a better future for all people in this country. It's a day for family, friends, and fireworks—and it can be a day for sharing fun facts too!

What's your favorite way to celebrate Independence Day?

GLOSSARY

American Civil War: A war fought from 1861 to 1865 in the United States between the Union (the Northern states) and the Confederacy (the Southern states).

anniversary: A date that is remembered or celebrated because a special event happened on that date in a previous year.

billion: 1,000 million, or 1,000,000,000.

celebrate: To honor with special activities.

Continental Congress: A group who represented the British North American colonies before, during, and after the American Revolution.

delegate: A person who acts on behalf of a group of people at an event.

design: The pattern or shape of something.

document: A formal piece of writing.

enslavement: The state of being forced to work without pay and treated as a piece of property.

statue: A likeness (like that of a person) made from a solid material such as marble or metal.

technology: Using science, engineering, and other industries to invent useful tools or to solve problems. Also a machine, piece of equipment, or method created by technology.

unity: The quality or state of being one and getting along.

FOR MORE INFORMATION

BOOKS

Bradley. Doug. *20 Things You Didn't Know About the Declaration of Independence.* Buffalo, NY: PowerKids Press, 2024.

Kesselring, Susan. *National Day Traditions Around the World.* Mankato, MN: The Child's World, 2022.

Taylor, Charlotte. *The Truth About Independence Day.* Buffalo, NY: Enslow Publishing, 2023.

WEBSITES

The Earliest July 4 Celebrations
www.mountvernon.org/george-washington/the-revolutionary-war/the-earliest-july-4-celebrations/
Find out more about the beginnings of this federal holiday.

The History of Fireworks
www.timeforkids.com/g56/history-fireworks
TIME for Kids offers a fun look back at this popular Fourth of July tradition.

Independence Day
kids.nationalgeographic.com/history/article/independence-day
National Geographic Kids explains the history of Independence Day.

Publisher's note to educators and parents: Our editors have carefully reviewed these websites to ensure that they are suitable for students. Many websites change frequently, however, and we cannot guarantee that a site's future contents will continue to meet our high standards of quality and educational value. Be advised that students should be closely supervised whenever they access the internet.

INDEX